FOKKER C.XIW

FLOATPLANE

Fokker C.XIw with registry W-4 is prepared on the catapult of HNLMS De Ruyter, shortly after arrival in the Netherlands Indies. (Collection: Navy Museum Den Helder)

The W-1 prototype is ready for a test flight. During testing, some edges of the fuselage panelling were taped over as a precautionary measure. The prototype featured a Scarff ring in the rear cockpit. (Collection: N. Braas)

A FOKKER CATAPULT PLANE FOR THE ROYAL NETHERLANDS NAVY

INTRODUCTION

In the pre-WWII years, a new generation of warships were built for the Royal Netherlands Navy. At first cruiser *De Ruyter* was built, followed by two larger cruisers (laid down in 1939) and even battlecruisers were considered.

Reconnaissance seaplanes designed to operate from these warships were needed. Aircraft that were suitable for use on the ship's catapult. Despite the availability of foreign aircraft, a plane designed and built by the national industry was preferred. Fokker, located in Amsterdam, was contacted.

De Ruyter was laid down on 16 September 1933 at the Wilton-Fijenoord dockyard in Schiedam and commissioned on 3 October 1936. She was sunk in the Battle of the Java Sea in 1942.

The Royal Netherlands Navy had formulated the following requirements for the new aircraft; high level of seaworthiness, landing speed of 82 km/hr and excellent manoeuvrability on the water. Maximum weight should not exceed 2400 kg with a useful load of 730 kg, and a range at cruise speed of at least 500 km was preferred. The new type was solely to serve as a reconnaissance aircraft and therefore no offensive armament (i.e. bomb racks) was required. If Fokker was able to offer a suitable design, an order of eight aircraft would be made. Fokker started design work on an aircraft intended as a reconnaissance catapult aircraft. Fokker presented the first studies to the Navy on 14 March 1934. This was a strengthened version of the Fokker C.VIIw, fitted with a 400 HP Lorraine 9N Algol nine-cylinder radial engine. The second proposed type was a Fokker C.X variant on floats which could be fitted with either an inline Rolls Royce Kestrel or radial engine. Neither type was accepted.

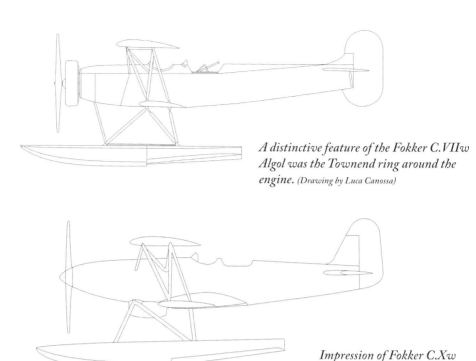

A distinctive feature of the Fokker C.VIIw Algol was the Townend ring around the engine. (Drawing by Luca Canossa)

Impression of Fokker C.Xw
(Drawing by Luca Canossa)

The prototype before a flight to Germany. Its civil registry is not yet applied, but the gun ring is removed, and the rear cockpit coaming is modified.
(Collection: N. Braas)

W-1 in its definitive form. Series production aircraft featured improved floats and a semi-enclosed cockpit.

FOKKER — A SHORT OVERVIEW

Dutchman Anthony Fokker learned how to build and fly aircraft while in Germany. His efforts brought great success when large amounts of aircraft were ordered by the German armed forces during the Great War. After the armistice Fokker diverted to his home country the Netherlands. His new aircraft company NV Nederlandsche Vliegtuigenfabriek (the name Fokker was at first avoided!) built several successful types during the interbellum, which were technically a continuation of the Fokker D.VII fighter. The military Fokker C.V biplane and civil transport Fokker F.VII were fundamental to the success of the company. Many new designs were careful improvements of these types.

A promotional image of W-4 flying above the Fokker works in Amsterdam.
(Collection: T. Postma)

Fokker continued to use the IDFLIEG system to name the aircraft types; C for reconnaissance, D for fighter, F for civil types and T for (torpedo)bomber. The letter was followed by a Roman number. The C.XIW dealt with in this title is Fokker's 11th reconnaissance type. The additional 'W' in the designation explains the type was a float plane.

FOKKER SHIPBORNE AIRCRAFT

During the early 1920s the Marineluchtvaart-dienst (Netherlands Fleet Air Arm) could muster an outdated fleet of about 15 floatplanes for sea reconnaissance. Discussions about the purchase of new aircraft started in 1922. Fokker responded with a variant of his successful Fokker C.IV fitted on floats, which turned out to be a failure.

A significantly more ambitious project was the B.II amphibian. It featured a metal flying boat hull housing a crew of three. The sesquiplane was powered by a 360 HP Rolls Royce Eagle IX engine. It was designed to be used from projected navy cruisers. After completing its test flights, it was offered to the navy for trials, but it did not meet expectations and was rejected.

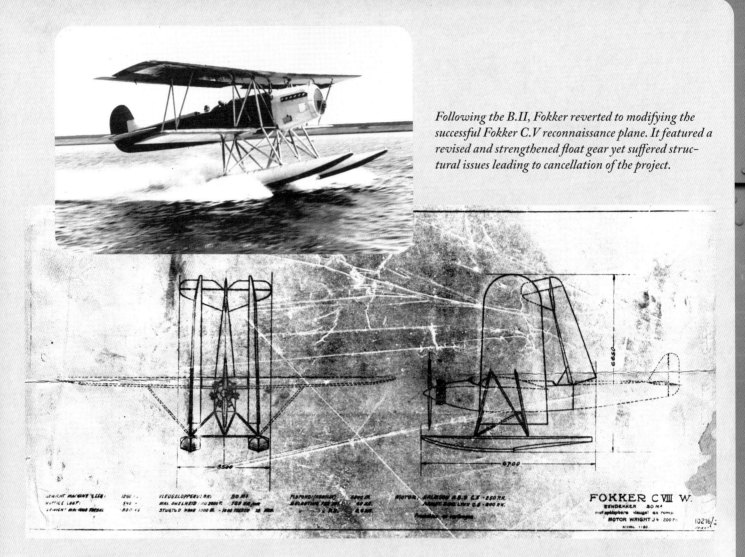

Following the B.II, Fokker reverted to modifying the successful Fokker C.V reconnaissance plane. It featured a revised and strengthened float gear yet suffered structural issues leading to cancellation of the project.

Following the failed Fokker bids to deliver suitable aircraft, the Dutch Navy purchased four Fairey IIID float planes for service aboard its new light cruisers. Another Fokker project, a variant of the Fokker C.VIIIw with radial engine and foldable wings, emerged in January 1927, but it never progressed beyond the drawing board.

Fokker received an order for delivery of 30 C.VIIw floatplanes, which were intended for service in the Netherlands and Netherlands Indies. The planes were primarily used as trainer aircraft, but due to a lack of alternatives, they were operated from ships as well. They were not suitable for catapult starts and had to be hoisted overboard by crane. Deliveries started in 1928. In April 1930 a C.VIIw was the first Dutch floatplane capable of performing a looping: quite a sight to behold for the surprised onlookers! Ten machines were still in service when war broke out in Europe. All were lost during strafing attacks by German aircraft. None of the Netherlands Indies machines remained in service before the start of the Japanese attacks.

(Collection: Netherlands Institute for Military History)

An early study dated 26 January 1935.

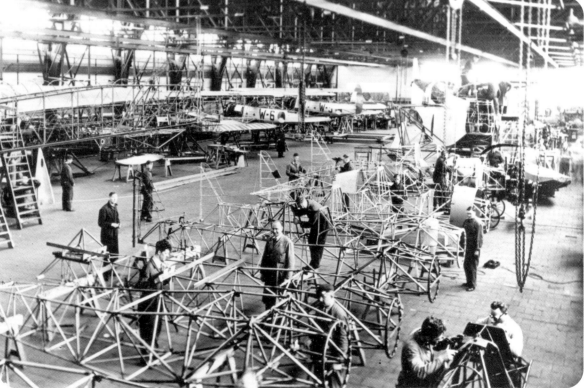

Production of different Fokker types, with four C.XIws in various stages of assembly. In front is the first series D.XXI intended for Finland. Behind those a Fokker T.IVA fuselage is seen.

Fokker proceeded with a completely new design, which was initially known as 'Ontwerp 120A*'. This was offered as type designation C.XIw on 3 May 1934. It was designed under the supervision of chief designer Marius Beeling, who had led the D.XVII and C.X design process earlier. The C.XIw could be fitted with a Kestrel inline engine or radial engine. This new design was favoured by the Navy, and during October Fokker was ordered to build a mock-up fuselage of both engine variants, to study the layout and view from the cockpit. This resulted in selecting an aircraft fitted with a Wright Cyclone radial engine and Fokker-built aluminium floats. After negotiating the terms and price, a contract was signed on 28 December 1934 for the delivery of one aircraft, at a price of Dfl. 80,000. The engine and instruments would be purchased separately. The prototype would be fitted with a Wright Cyclone SR 1820-F2 engine of 762 HP at 800 metres. The aircraft needed to be finished before 15 July 1935.

Quickly after reaching an agreement, construction started. The Fokker C.XIw was built according to the company's usual construction methods; the fuselage was a welded tubular frame which was partially covered by aluminium panels. A 440-litre fuel tank and 42-litre oil tank were placed between the engine and crew. The Cyclone engine was covered with NACA cowls and propelled a wooden Weybridge propeller.

Left: A craftsman is working on the welded tubular frame fuselage. An assembly jig is still attached to the fuselage side. The float undercarriage was welded to the fuselage.

Right: The synchronised FN Browning machine gun was easily accessible. A small window can be seen behind the hatches.

In the front of the picture a pair of lower wings can be seen, with three top wings behind. In the background, Fokker T.V wings are being built, which also included the fuselage centre section.

A fixed FN Browning 7.7 mm machine gun with 500 rounds was fitted in the port side of the fuselage.
The observer operated a movable FN Browning 7.7 mm machine gun. Five boxes with 100 rounds of ammunition were stored below the gun.

The wooden wings were built according to typical Fokker construction; they featured two spruce box spars and plywood ribs with birch capstrips. The wings were partially covered with plywood and fully covered with linen. The top wing was constructed as a single piece and featured ailerons. The centre of the top wing contained two storage bays which held hoisting attachments. They were covered with easily closable metal hatches. The lower wings were built in halves and featured flaps. The C.XIw had a large wing surface of 40 m² and a relatively low wing loading of 60 kg m². Interestingly, the C.XIw was not fitted with a landing light. There were no provisions to carry a bomb load or flares.

---

* Fokker had started using *Ontwerp* numbers in 1934, which were used to distinguish design projects

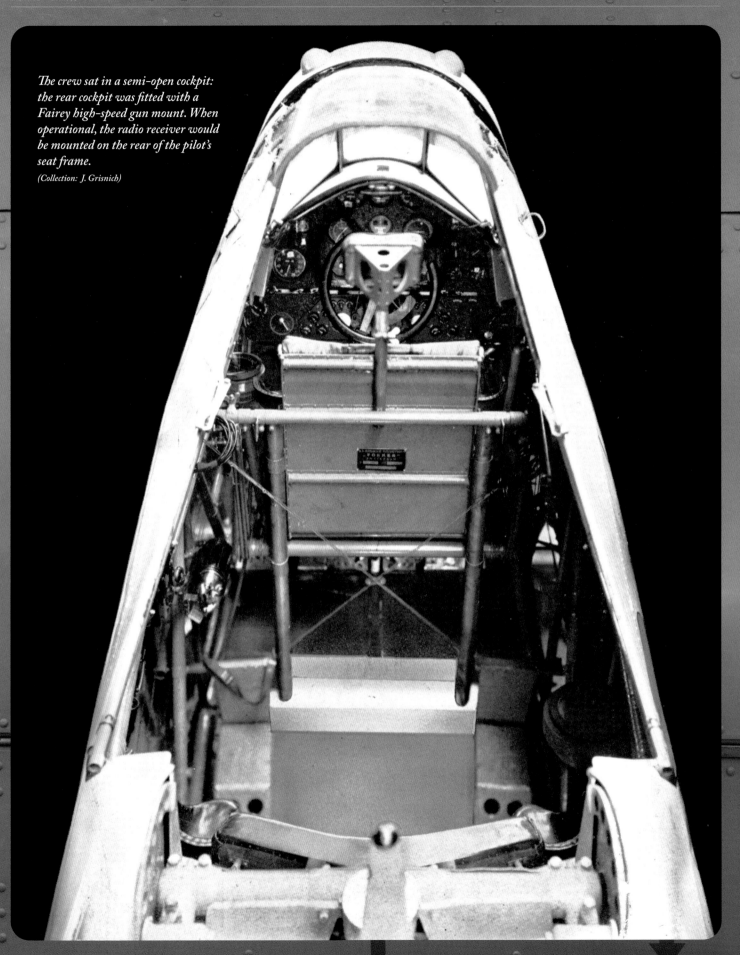

The crew sat in a semi-open cockpit: the rear cockpit was fitted with a Fairey high-speed gun mount. When operational, the radio receiver would be mounted on the rear of the pilot's seat frame.
(Collection: J. Grisnich)

With panels removed, the fuselage was easily accessible for maintenance and repairs.

After completion of the main components, the prototype was lifted aboard a barge and during the night of 8 to 9 July it was transported to Marine Vliegkamp (Dutch abbreviation MVK - Naval Air Station, NAS) Schellingwoude near Amsterdam. Here, it would be assembled and made ready for the first flight. Fokker test pilot Emil Meinecke took off for the first flight during the early morning of 20 July 1935, and Navy pilot-officer Van der Kroeff made a second flight during the same morning. The first flights were considered a success. During take-off on July 25th the W-1 cut through high waves, causing damage to two of the float struts, which required repair and strengthening. Some modification work was done while the prototype was at the Fokker works. The plane was back in the air on 7 August. The remainder of the test programme proceeded without trouble. The most notable modification was the fitting of a new tail rudder of increased size, to improve the taxiing performance. Poor weather on 30 October prevented delivery of the plane.

The prototype had to be brought to MVK Schellingwoude by barge: a 5 km trip across het IJ, a wide channel directly north of Amsterdam.

The W-1 being towed out of the hangar at MVK Schell-ingwoude.

Bottom: The landing performance was tested on 20 August, during which the W-1 flew with high visibility markings on the lower wing tips. This was done during trials which were filmed for research purposes.

TRIALS

The C.XIw would now be prepared for the next stage of the flight testing, which would take place in Warnemünde, Germany. The temporary civil registry *PH-ALC* was allotted on 12 November 1935. Pilot-officer Van der Kroeff, accompanied by Fokker engineer Stok, would fly the plane to Warnemünde. Here, the C.XIw would be subjected to catapult take-off trials at the Heinkel proving grounds. The two men left Schellingwoude on 9 December. The catapult trials were executed by Royal Netherlands Navy pilots van der Kroeff and Bakker and Heinkel chief test pilot Nitschke. After the trials had been successfully concluded the plane returned to MVK (Naval Air Station) Schellingwoude on 10 January 1936.

W-1 was disarmed for its trip to Warnemünde. The gun ring was removed, and the cockpit coaming of the rear cockpit was temporarily modified.

(Collection: P. Staal)

W-1, now with civilian registry PH-ALC *is positioned on the catapult. The catapult itself was placed on a river barge.*
(Collection: P. Staal)

In just half a second, the C.XIw is catapulted to 105 km/hr. (Collection: P. Staal)

The prototype was now returned to the Fokker works for further modifications. A semi-enclosed cockpit hood was fitted, covering the pilot's cockpit. The gun ring in the rear cockpit was replaced with a more refined Fairey high-speed gun mount. These features were very similar to those of the Fokker C.X reconnaissance plane, which was just leaving the production line. The W-1 was again released for further catapult trials, now fitted with the new cockpit enclosure.

New, considerably more refined, aluminium floats were designed by Fokker. The design of the new floats was completed during April 1936 and con-

Test pilot Emil Meinecke is seen here in the modified cockpit, accompanied by Fokker engineer Slot.

(Collection: T. Postma)

Construction of the refined aluminium floats, and a completed example.

A modified W-1 *performing a test.*

Bottom:
HNLMS **De Ruyter** *just after the commissioning ceremony. Her function was to aid the existing cruisers in the defence of the Dutch East Indies. Trials showed that her stackcap was not satisfactory, and was replaced by another one as pictured.*

(Collection: Navy Museum Den Helder)

struction started at once. After completion and fitting of the floats, the *W-1* resumed flying on 9 September 1936. The prototype was again tested during sea trials, which commenced on 14 September 1936. The new float construction proved satisfactory. A rudder was fitted to one of them, which vastly improved manoeuvrability on the water. The aircraft's performance in general had improved after the modifications.

Landing characteristics were found to be excellent, although the prescribed landing speed was increased to 100 km/hr. The prototype was equipped with landing flaps, but these proved to be unnecessary. The series production aircraft would not be fitted with them, and *W-1* would be retrofitted with a new set of lower wings without flaps. All extra work on the prototype had caused a large budget overrun. Fokker had spent Dfl. 145,000 on design, construction, and modification

work. Fokker was fully compensated, and the prototype was officially handed over to the Navy.

The *W-1* was sent to Den Helder on 9 October 1936, to be aboard the HNLMS *De Ruyter* when the ship would be commissioned. The crew was surprised by fog and had to make a precautionary landing near the town of Medemblik. The plane was taxied to nearby port "Oude Zeug" and put under guard. Despite the delay, the *W-1* was embarked when the cruiser was commissioned on 13 October 1936.

SEA TRIALS

After its return to Holland, the *W-1* underwent further seaworthy trials on 21 January. The *W-1* was first launched from HNLMS *De Ruyter*'s catapult on 7 May 1936. The ship had just returned from her first sea trials and steamed just past the jetty of Den Helder navy port to allow the plane a take-off opportunity.

Some impressions of the first catapult trials on cruiser De Ruyter. *The ship's funnel was later modified because it was covering the ship with soot.* (Top: Collection: J. Mulder)

The W-1 being hoisted back aboard. During the catapult trials a metal windshield was placed in front of the rear cockpit.

HNLMS De Ruyter *during the trials, with the original funnel. Photographed off the Scottish coast, summer 1936.*
(Collection: Netherlands Institute for Military History)

CRUISER DE RUYTER AND ITS CATAPULT

A rock-steady trust in the Netherlands' neutrality and international treaties influenced the size and effectiveness of the fleet in the Netherlands East Indies (Indonesia). The navy never possessed powerful battleships and laws accepted in 1927 saw to it that there were no more than two light cruisers as heaviest ships; HNLMS *Java* and *Sumatra*. A third, *Celebes*, was cancelled while it was under construction. The economic crisis of the early 1930s thwarted ambitious new purchases. In 1931. funds for a third light cruiser of a new design were finally allotted.

Despite serious opposition from the navy top brass, a strict budget only allowed one light cruiser of 6600 tons with seven main guns of 150 mm. The ship was built by Wilton-Fijenoord in just over two years. Launched in 1935 and one year later commissioned as HNLMS *De Ruyter*. The use of electric welding and some light alloy provided better weight economy in the design. Despite her small displacement, *De Ruyter* was fitted with several noteworthy systems. It featured an anti-aircraft armament of 5 twin stabilised 40 mm Bofors mountings, fitted with a highly advanced fire control system. *De Ruyter* was propelled by three modern two-stage steam turbines which provided economic low-speed performance and a very favourable top speed. Although she was somewhat restricted in her main armament, she was a fast ship, reaching 33.5 knots on trials.

The boiler uptakes were all led to a single funnel with a prominent smoke deflector,. On each side, were cranes for handling the aircraft and boats stowed on deck.

The reserve plane was placed between the catapult and the anti-aircraft batteries. (Collection: Navy Museum Den Helder)

De Ruyter was to act as squadron leader and had a wartime task scouting and intercepting enemy ships. For this task the ship was to be fitted with a catapult system and two reconnaissance aircraft. One aircraft needed to be placed on the catapult, while the second was placed on a small deck aft of the catapult. The second aircraft was already placed on its catapult sled and could easily be rolled on to the catapult.

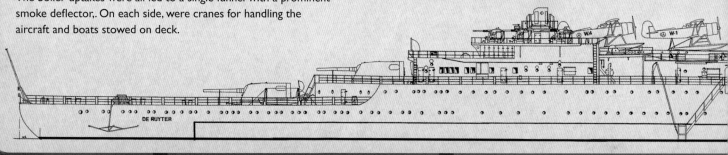

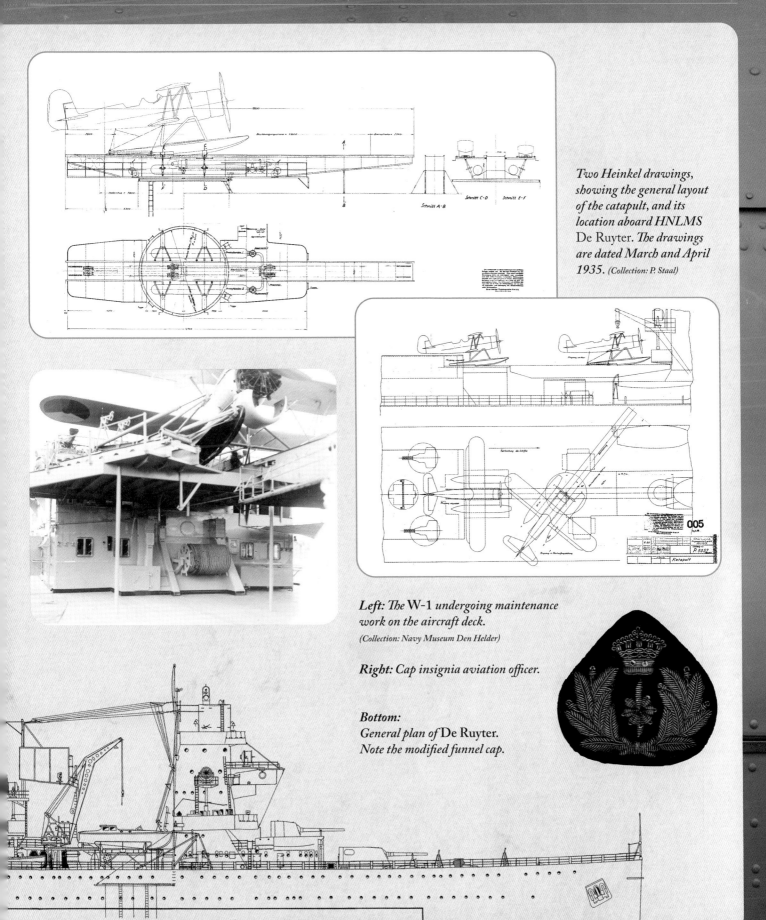

Two Heinkel drawings, showing the general layout of the catapult, and its location aboard HNLMS De Ruyter. The drawings are dated March and April 1935. (Collection: P. Staal)

Left: *The W-1 undergoing maintenance work on the aircraft deck.*
(Collection: Navy Museum Den Helder)

Right: *Cap insignia aviation officer.*

Bottom:
General plan of De Ruyter. Note the modified funnel cap.

The new cruiser started trials on 27 April 1936. She returned for a short maintenance stop and commenced catapult trials on 7th of May.

After a docking period in Rotterdam, *De Ruyter* made a two-week journey to the Scottish coasts, during which the catapult was tested with a dummy weight, equalling that of a fully laden Fokker C.XIw.
After commissioning, the ship had a crew of 435 men. A group of eight were dispatched for service and maintenance of the aircraft and handling the catapult and crane.

The Heinkel catapult is prepared for the first tests, May 1936.

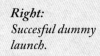

Right:
Succesful dummy launch.

Left and righ:
HNLMS De Ruyter *with* W-1 *aboard, shortly before her departure to the Netherlands Indies.*
(Collection: Navy Museum Den Helder)

The aircraft rested on the catapult on a launching carriage with four supports. (Collection: Navy Museum Den Helder)

Dutch warships had been equipped with aircraft from the 1920s but none of them had been fitted with a catapult before. The German Heinkel K-8 compressed air catapult, weighing 10000 kg, was selected, and was placed between the funnel and aft deck house. The 18.70-metre-long catapult ramp was placed on a turntable which could be swung 90 degrees outboard either with a manually operated crank or electric motor. The catapult launch system was operated with compressed air which was held in two 850-litre storage cylinders located alongside of the catapult. Outlet pressure of 85 atmosphere allowed for a quick acceleration to 40 metres per second. The catapult could launch aircraft of maximum 3000 kg take-off weight, which would reach 105 km/h take-off speed in just over half a second. The aircraft would be launched within 16 metres. When the aircraft had been launched, the last 2.7 metres of the catapult ramp were needed to decelerate the aircraft sled. This was realised by a brake piston filled with a mixture of water and glycerine.

(Collection: Navy Museum Den Helder)

The catapult start

Before the plane could be launched it would be warming up the engine as usual. The catapult officer gave the order to swing the catapult outboard. The ship itself set out a course and speed, allowing the aircraft a favourable headwind for take-off. After measuring the wind speed, the necessary pressure was selected by the catapult officer. When he gave the all-clear, the pilot prepared for launch. He closed the cockpit hood, braced his head against the head rest and positioned his arms firmly on the arm rests of his seat. With his feet on the rudders, he selected full engine power. A tap on the side window was the pilot's sign that he was ready for launch. The observer in the rear cockpit similarly prepared for launch. He sat in a seat with a low back rest; the Fairey high speed gun ring featured a head rest for bracing.

After the pilot quickly made final preparations, and three seconds after his hand disappeared from sight, the catapult officer activated the catapult.

The C.XIw had to be landed as close to the ship as possible. Afterwards it could be picked up by the ship's crane at a maximum speed of 12 knots/hr. De Ruyter was fitted with two 13-meter-high electrically operated cranes, which were needed to pick up landed aircraft. The cranes were fitted with a stabilizer to compensate for the seaway of the ship, allowing for a smooth hoisting of the aircraft.

(Collection: T. Postma)

The observer had to crawl out of his cockpit, scramble over the pilot's cockpit enclosure and hook up a sling to four attachments on the top of the upper wing. The engine had to be kept running during this procedure and could be switched off only when the pick-up was success-fully completed.
W-8, seen here, is fitted with a radio. Two short antennae were fitted to the wing tips. An aerial was connected between them and the vertical tail (Collection: T. Postma)

Aircraft pick-up

After it had been hoisted out of the water, the plane could be placed on the catapult, or the decking directly aft of the catapult. When the aircraft was back on board it had to be hosed down with fresh water to prevent corrosion.

W-1 was aboard cruiser *De Ruyter* when she left for the Netherlands Indies on 12 January 1937. When not flying, the fuselage was covered by a large black tarpaulin. During the first leg of the journey, the *W-1* remained aboard HNLMS *De Ruyter*. After going through the Suez Canal there was finally time for training flights while steaming through the Red Sea. *De Ruyter* arrived at her home base Surabaya on Saturday 13 March.

Shortly after *De Ruyter* had departed for the Netherlands Indies, Fokker received a production order for eight aircraft. Contracts were signed on 26 January 1937 - nearly three years after the design work had started! With the *W-1* no longer available for test work, further development of the C.XIw type had to wait until a new machine was completed. Based on experiences with the *W-1*, the series production aircraft were fitted with a

Emil Meinecke, left, and Frans Stok, right, in front of the first series production aircraft.

W-5 was displayed during the "Avia" aviation fair which was held in the Hague between 30 July and 15 August 1937. Another of the new aircraft was displayed during the air defence day at Scheveningen on 21 August.

slightly more powerful Wright Cyclone SR 1820-F52 engine, rated at 775 HP. They did not have landing flaps fitted in the lower wings. The observer's cockpit was enlarged by 10 centimetres, allowing for a bit more workspace. The series production aircraft were armed similarly to the prototype. A Nedinsco* 4A reflex sight was fitted behind the windshield. Otherwise,

the aircraft were similar to the prototype. The series aircraft were registered *W-2* to *W-9* (c/n. 5420 to 5427). The first four aircraft were delivered during June 1937. Two aircraft were delivered in August and another two in December. *W-3* was kept at Fokker for test work and was finally delivered on 12 February 1938.

In the meantime, two 'flotilla leaders' (light cruisers) had been ordered. *Tromp* and *Jacob van Heemskerck* would be equipped with one Fokker C.XIw each. Because of their smaller displacement, they lacked a catapult.

---

* Nedinsco was a Dutch company located in Venlo. It produced Carl Zeiss optical sights, binoculars, and suchlike. The 4A sight mentioned was most likely an early REVI product.

Assembly drawing dated 16 September 1936.	
Wingspan (upper wing)	13.00 m
Wingspan (lower wing)	11.50 m
Length	10.45 m
Height	4.50 m
Wing surface	40 m²
Empty weight	1770 kg
Payload	780 kg
Total weight	2550 kg
Top speed (sea level)	262 km/h
Top speed (1800 m)	276 km/h
Cruise speed (sea level)	233 km/h
Cruise speed (1800 m)	248 km/h
Rate of climb	
To 1000 m	2.35 m
To 2000 m	4.7 m
To 3000 m	7.7 m
To 4000 m	11.0 m
To 5000 m	16.6 m
To 6000 m	22.0 m
To 6500 m	25.0 m
Practical ceiling	6500 m
Absolute ceiling	6850 m
Flight range (cruise speed)	440 km
Flight range (economic speed)	610 km
Take-off length from water	500-700 m

W-15 was the final production machine, and was taken into service on 18 January 1938. It is seen here at MVK de Mok. (Collection: Navy Museum Den Helder)

Because of the planned new ships, a second contract for six additional aircraft was signed on 11 October 1937. These were registered *W-10* to *W-15* (c/n. 5461 to 5466). This contract included two spare floats, two spare engine cowls and other spare parts. The first two aircraft were in fact already handed over on 8 October, two more were delivered in December 1937, and the final pair on 18 January 1938.

Three aircraft were to remain in the Netherlands for training. Besides the earlier mentioned ships, Fokker C.XIws would be used aboard the older light cruisers HNLMS *Java* and *Sumatra*. Both ships could carry two aircraft each. The gun boats HNLMS *Soemba* and *Flores* were able to carry one machine on the aft deck. If all ships were at sea simultaneously, ten would be aboard ships, leaving only two in reserve…

HNLMS Tromp *shortly after completion. (Collection: Netherlands Institute for Military History)*

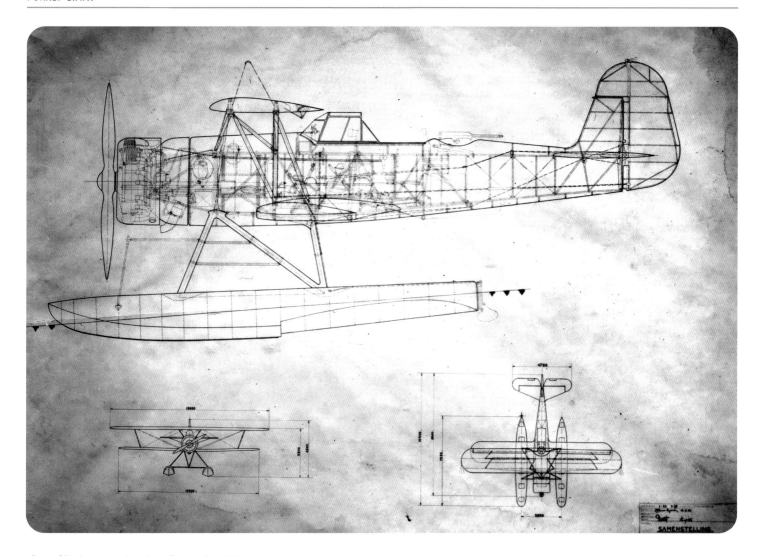

Assembly drawing dated 16 September 1936.

W-5 as it was displayed during the Avia aviation fair of the Hague. (Colour profile by Luca Canossa)

COLOURS AND MARKINGS

The fuselage and wings of the aircraft were painted in an aluminium dope finish, which conserved the aircraft's linen covering in tropical conditions. All struts and the top of the floats were painted in *Hollandgrijs* (also documented as Holland-grau, translated as Holland grey). This was a grey-greenish hue, RLM63 (later renumbered as RLM02) in the German RLM paint system). Upon delivery, the bottoms of the floats were painted black. This was later replaced with a glossy aluminium finish. The red-white-blue roundels were placed on the wing surfaces and on the fuselage, while the rudder was also painted in the national colours.

W-10 *aboard HNLMS* Tromp.
Note the black markings on the leading edges of the wings, which indicated wing strengthenings, allowing for manhandling the plane when it was hoisted aboard. (Collection: Jt. Mulder)

When, on 4 May 1938, HNLMS Java *departed for the Netherlands Indies,* W-15 *was embarked.*
There was room for two aircraft and ammo (80 bombs of 50 kilos and 8,000 rounds for its guns).

Bottom
W-3 is prepared for departure from MVK de Mok.
Collection: N. Braas)

The aircraft were placed on trestles. The lower half of the engine cowling remained suspended with cables during maintenance.

(Collection: Navy Museum Den Helder)

SERVICE IN HOLLAND

After delivery most of the aircraft were crated and sent to the Netherlands Indies by ship. Cruiser HNLMS *Java* was in Holland for modification work during delivery of the Fokkers. After completion of this work, *Java* performed escort tasks near Gibraltar in February and made a visit to Denmark in March *.

W-3, *W-9* and *W-14* were to remain in Holland and used for training purposes. For this purpose, the aircraft were fitted with dual controls.

---

*   During the Spanish civil war various European navies escorted shipping through the Strait of Gibraltar

W-6 *on the ramp of MVK (Naval Air Station) Schellingwoude on an artificial island east of Amsterdam.*
(Collection: T. Postma)

The three C.XIw's moored at the small auxiliary station of Alkmaardermeer. Interestingly, W-9 is fitted with a pair of old floats. (Collection: N. Braas)

W-10 *hoisted onboard.*

(Collection: Navy Museum Den Helder)

A fourth aircraft was temporarily stationed in Holland, when W-10 returned home aboard cruiser Sumatra on 26 July 1938. Between 10 October and 10 December HNLMS Sumatra made a goodwill voyage with W-10 aboard, visiting several ports in Portugal (including Madeira), French Morocco and Gibraltar.

(Collection: T. Postma)

W-9 was used for shipboard trials when the new light cruiser Tromp was undergoing her sea trials. (Collection: N. Braas)

Embarked on a smaller ship, like HNLMS Tromp here, meant careful ship manoeuvring in tidy waters. Because the wingtips protruded, aircraft handling had to be done with a boom, while a boat winch was provided for the required lifting power. (Collection: Navy Museum Den Helder)

During the second half of the 1930s, Fokker created several designs for maritime use. Three of these designs were accepted and ordered by the Royal Netherlands Navy.

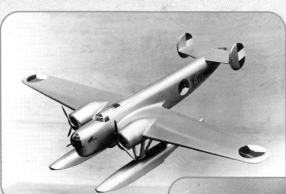

Ontwerp 125

A large twin-engine bomber on floats

Fokker invested a lot of time in the design for a T.IV successor. *Ontwerp 125* was a navalised variant of the Fokker T.V land bomber, which would first be offered to the Dutch navy as Fokker T.VIIw during October 1935. A revised design, discussed a year later, did not meet expectations.

A proposed single-engine torpedo bomber

During 1936 a successor to the C.VIIIw was discussed. Fokker designed *Ontwerp 131*, a single-engine parasol-wing monoplane for a crew of three. It would be powered by a Wright Cyclone R-1820 F52 engine and was to be fitted with torpedo shackles. A series of six aircraft was offered as C.XIIIw on 3 December 1936. An order never materialised.

Purchase of Fokker C.XIVw

A series of 24 Fokker C.XIVw machines was ordered during January 1939. They were trainer aircraft, intended to replace the obsolete C.VIIw. All aircraft were delivered during the same year. The first production aircraft is seen here with the first Fokker T.VIIIw.

A twin-engine torpedo bomber

Following the discussion on C.XIIIw, a new torpedo bomber was created during early 1937. This design, *Ontwerp 134*, would evolve into the Fokker T.VIIIw. An order for twenty-four examples of mixed construction, followed by 12 all-metal machines. Only nine of the first mentioned variant could be delivered before war broke out on 10 May 1940.

Torpedo bomber study

During January 1939 a single-engined torpedo bomber was drawn. The floatplane design received *Ontwerp* number 169. If ordered, it would enter service as T.Xw.

Strengthening of the fleet

During November 1938, strengthening of the fleet returned on the political agenda. With the increasing threat of war in both Europe and Asia, a plan was devised to build new ships in the battle cruiser class. After long debates, the decision was taken to build three (or four) battlecruisers with nine 28 cm guns as main armament, increase speed to 32 miles and total displacement of 27,000 tons. The new ships would be equipped with a catapult and up to four aircraft. The new ships would need to be a match for the Japanese *Kongo*-class battlecruisers.

Fokker C.XVw – a successor to C.XIw

While discussion on the new battlecruisers was taking place, the Dutch navy was looking into a replacement for the C.XIw, Fokker was contacted during August 1939.

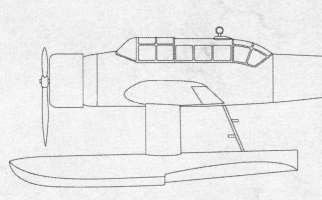

This new type had to be an all-metal monoplane for a crew of three. The navy anticipated an initial order for six aircraft. *Ontwerp 194* was developed, which at first glance was quite similar to the earlier *Ontwerp 169*, but capable of being catapulted. Design work progressed and on 30 December the type received designation C.XVw. The fuselage layout was revised several times and Fokker made performance calculations based on three engine types.

Discussions for a potential order now entered an advanced stage. A contract for a prototype was drawn up, with a clause for an order of five aircraft if the type was accepted. When the Netherlands was attacked on 10 May 1940, all work on the design was terminated.

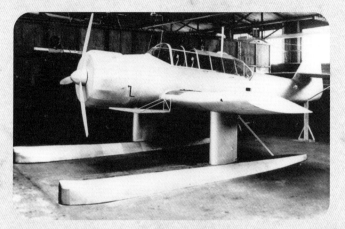

A mock-up was constructed and on 6 February 1940 reviewed by a delegation of the navy. The mock-up was modified and received a single streamlined float strut. This variant was presented on 1 March.

Technical details (in reconnaissance role, as calculated on 2 April 1940)	
Engine	Wright Cyclone GR 1820 G102A, 900 HP
Wingspan (upper wing)	14.00 m
Length	11.30 m
Height	4.70 m
Wing surface	32 m²
Empty weight	2400 kg
Payload	1100 kg
Total weight	3500 kg
Top speed	338 km/h
Cruise speed	244 km/h

Rate of climb		
	To 1000 m	2.25 min
	To 2000 m	4.55 min
	To 3000 m	7.1 min
	To 4000 m	10.3 min
	To 5000 m	14.7 min
	To 6000 m	21.7 min

Practical ceiling	6550 m
Absolute ceiling	6900 m
Flight range	1080 km
Armament	2 fixed 7.7 mm FN Browning machine guns with 350 rounds per gun in the wings. 1 flexibly mounted 7.7 mm FN Browning machine gun in the rear cockpit with 5 x 100 rounds, 200 kg bombs.

W-9 *seen at MVK (Naval Air Station) Schellingwoude.*

(Collection: T. Postma)

Following the Italian invasion of Albania on 7 April 1939, Dutch armed forces mobilised as a precautionary measure.. The three aircraft were used in a quickly formed GVT (Groep Vliegtuigen, or Aircraft Group). The aircraft were normally based at MVK de Mok, located on the island of Texel but during this mobilisation the group relocated to MVK Schellingwoude. After the mobilisation was suspended, the aircraft were ordered to return to MVK de Mok on 18 April. (Collection T. Postma)

W-14 turned over during take-off on 18 April. 1939. The heavily damaged aircraft was sent to Fokker for repairs.

On 5 December 1938, a royal decree was signed which resulted in painting over the national colours on the tail planes of all military aircraft. This measure would decrease visibility of aircraft on the water, and in the air. The rudders of the C.XIw were painted over with aluminium coloured paint. (Colour profile by Luca Canossa)

W-10 left Holland again aboard the newly commissioned HNLMS *Tromp* on 19 August 1939. The light cruiser had left during a period of rising international tensions. Fears of German aggression led to a full mobilisation on 29 August 1939 – just days before Germany invaded Poland on 1 September. HNLMS *Sumatra*, still in the Netherlands, started her coastal patrol work, but lacked an aircraft for the remaining time she stayed in Europe.

The United Kingdom and France declared war on Germany on 3 September, which was swiftly followed by the Dutch recon-firmation of its neutrality. On the same day German offensive flying activities commenced against English navy vessels.

Sailing to the east, HNLMS Tromp *executed several exercises. Along the Portuguese coast this included reconnaissance by the* W-10. *The ship continued its journey via Gibraltar, the Suez Canal and Sabang - the first port in the Netherlands East Indies. (Collection: Jt. Mulder)*

The W-9, *which was lost during the night of 13 April. It is seen here at MVK de Mok.* (Collection: T. Postma)

Flying boats and floatplanes, heading for England, navigated along the Dutch coast, often very close to the 3-mile zone. In response, the Netherlands Naval Aviation Service started flying patrol flights along the North Sea coast.

This patrol flying resulted in some early confrontations. A Fokker T.VIIIw floatplane was shot down by German aircraft on 13 September 1939. The Dutch roundel,

with its segments of red, white, and blue (and orange centre), was apparently misidentified as being a British or French one. The T.VIIIw was lost during this confrontation. As response to the affair a new highvisible nationality marking was deemed necessary, to prevent further misidentifications and to emphasize Dutch neutrality. A first proposal was made on the day after the incident, which entailed painting over the roundels with a black-rimmed

orange ball. Although the proposal was not accepted, the orange ball did appear on several Fokker C.VIIw planes. A new proposal was filed, which was accepted. An equilateral orange triangle with a 10-centimetre black rim would be placed on the middle of the wing surfaces. The size of the triangle would have to be 80% of the wing chord. A black-rimmed orange triangle had to be placed on the middle of the rear fuselage. The tail rudder, finally, had to be painted orange, with a 10 centimetre black border, as well. All markings had to be painted over before 1 October 1939 0h00.

W-3 *with the new highly-visible nationality markings. The observer's gun is fitted, and the pilot's Nedinsco 4A reflex sight is just visible. Interestingly, the C.XIw was the only Dutch military aircraft with a modern optical sight.* (Collection: T. Postma)

The W-9, which was lost during the night of 13 April. It is seen here at MVK de Mok.
(Collection: T. Postma)

Pilot's recollections

Netherlands Fleet Air Arm (MLD) pilot P.J. Elias wrote a book about his flying career titled *"Dan liever de lucht in"*, which was first published in 1963. Elias was stationed in the Netherlands Indies and was on leave in the Netherlands when the armed forces were mobilised. In his memoires he also mentions flights in the Fokker C.XIw. He was ordered to report at Naval Air Station de Mok;

"Our orders were to fly patrols during the morning and afternoon, following the coastline of the northern part of the Netherlands, from the city of IJmuiden all the way up to Rottum Island and vice versa. We had to make sure the three-mile zone was respected by the combatant nations.

We kept flying during all weather conditions. This was not very comfortable, especially during winter. I had just returned from the tropics, so the cold climate above the North Sea was a huge transition for me. The sight of the stormy waters below was enough to give me the shivers. The ice-cold slip stream which rushed past our cockpit did the rest. I had an old fur coat sewn into the inside of my uniform and squeezed in some old newspapers between my uniform and flight coverall for protection against the cold."

---

*   Translation: Then I'd Rather Take to the Air

The *W-14* had been repaired and could join the other aircraft in the Groep Vliegtuigen, now baptised GVT 3. Flying conditions during the last months of 1939 were very poor, which limited flying to the bare minimum. On 6 December a German mine laying operation, involving 29 aircraft, resulted in various violations of Dutch neutrality. Two Heinkel He 59 floatplanes made emergency landings close to the Dutch islands Terschelling and Ameland. Various German aircraft and patrol boats were sent to the stranded aircraft. After a while, Dutch aircraft were sent to investigate the situation near Ameland. Two Fokker C.VIIIws from MVK Schellingwoude and a Fokker C.XIw from MVK de Mok arrived over the scene, as did a patrol of three Fokker D.XXI fighters. Before the situation escalated further, the stranded aircraft were quickly towed to neutral waters. A pair of Fokker T.VIIIw floatplanes armed with bombs, and cruiser *Sumatra*, steaming towards the scene, retreated without attacking.

The group moved to MVK Schellingwoude, but due to the extreme winter conditions service at MVK Schellingwoude became impossible. GVT 3 transferred to MVK Veere in January 1940, which remained operational due to the brackish water there. But severe cold ultimately prevented any further flying. Koolhoven F.K. 51 trainers had to temporarily take over the patrol duties until spring set in.

GVT 3 returned to MVK de Mok during the spring of 1940, and coastal patrol work continued by day and by night. Following the German invasion of Norway on 7 April, all branches of the military were on high alert. During the early evening of 13 April, a German convoy of 16 ships was reported off the coast of Den Helder. An invasion was feared and three Dutch submarines were hurriedly ordered to take up positions. An MLD crew was ordered to locate the convoy with Fokker C.XIw *W-9* during the night. The crew of *W-9* must have experienced difficulties. Coast guard officers witnessed how the plane disappeared into the North Sea near Kamperduin. Although a jetty was launched, the crew members sergeant pilot Knaapen and lieutenant Langenhoff could not be rescued.

W-14, after it had been repaired. The 'W' had been painted out to create room for the triangle marking.

(Collection: T. Postma)

10 MAY 1940

When the Netherlands was attacked by Germany, the two remaining C.XIws were part of GVT 3. The *W-3* was not operational though, as it was undergoing repairs at MVK de Mok. The *W-14* was located at GVT 3's base at MVK (Naval Air Station) Veere. Four Fokker C.XIVw floatplanes were added to GVT 3; *F-17* and *F-23* were operational, *F-21* and *F-24* were in reserve. Another aircraft group, GVT 6, was based at MVK Veere with three Fokker C.VIIIw floatplanes.

Order of battle:

Trainers

15	Koolhoven F.K.51
15	Fokker S.IX
10	Fokker C.VIIw
24	Fokker C.XIVw

Reconnaissance aircraft

9	Fokker C.VIIIw
2	Fokker C.XIw
8	Fokker T.VIIIw

The *W-14* made one patrol flight on 10 May, during which the crew encountered German aircraft. Combat could be avoided and the C.XIw escaped without trouble. MVK Veere was not attacked during the first day of war, but MVK de Mok was. C.XIw *W-3* was destroyed in the main hangar of the base. HNLMS *Sumatra* was in the port of Vlissingen on 10 May. She escaped being bombed and fled to England, but without a C.XIw aboard. Light cruiser *Jacob van Heemskerck*, which was still under construction, was launched in a rush, commissioned, and prepared for evacuation to England. With a tugboat, the ship departed in the evening of 10 May, but without a plane aboard. On 12 May, a formation of Heinkel He 111 bombers caused some damage on MVK Veere. The C.XIVw F-21 was destroyed, while *F-24* was heavily damaged.

MVK de Mok was heavily damaged during German attacks. The wreck of **W-3** *seen in the hangar, with a C.VIIw and C.XIVw.*

(Collection: Netherlands Institute for Military History)

Many MLD aircraft had been destroyed or damaged during the first days of the war, and it was clear the role of the MLD was over. Preparations were made to evacuate the remaining aircraft to France. The *W-14* left Veere during the morning of 14 May, together with five Fokker C.VIIIws and eleven Fokker C.XIVws. After a two-hour flight Boulogne sur Mer was reached, and later that day the aircraft continued to Cherbourg. After contemplating some form of cooperation with the French, it was decided to carry on to the United Kingdom. The aircraft took off on 22 May and reached Calshot, on the Solent, without trouble. There was no use for the aircraft there, so the *W-14* was crated and shipped to the Netherlands Indies.

The light cruisers HNLMS *Jacob van Heemskerck* (completed in the UK) and *Sumatra* were ordered to evacuate the royal family to Canada and left the British port of Milford Haven during the evening of 2 June 1940 – again without aircraft on board. After fulfilling this task, HNLMS *Sumatra* performed patrol tasks in the Caribbean, during which she hunted for a German raider, east of the Leeward Antilles. The lack of its shipboard aircraft must have been frustrating the hunt. The *Sumatra* returned to the Netherlands Indies via Cape Town, South Africa, on 27 September.

During operational use the black bottoms of the floats were repainted with aluminium coloured paint.

(Collection: Navy Museum Den Helder)

SERVICE IN THE NETHERLANDS INDIES

After the arrival of HNLMS *De Ruyter* in the Netherlands Indies a three-month period of training commenced. The ship's crew had to master many disciplines, including catapult operations. During peace time, the C.XIw crews formed the long-range reconnaissance of the fleet. The crews had to monitor (foreign) shipping activity but were also on the lookout for piracy, smuggling and other unusual activities. For this task, the C.XIw was equipped with 5-metre HF radio equipment. During artillery drills, the observer also acted as spotter and could provide guidance using radio. Another important task was target towing, which offered the anti-aircraft gunners a practice target. Four aircraft were fitted with a winch, which was placed aft of the observer's cockpit. The target drogue was towed with a 1000-metre-long cable.

W-1 *seen on the ramp of MVK Morokrembangan.* (Via K. Kalkman)

Shortly after arrival and unboxing of the first C.XIws, two were embarked on HNLMS *Sumatra*. The planes were immediately involved in a major week-long exercise, which commenced on 1 September 1937. Both aircraft were airborne on the second day of the exercise and ordered to scout for submarine activity. The aircraft were also given more modest tasks, such as transporting the mail to shore. HNLMS *Sumatra* returned to the Netherlands, leaving port on 8 June 1938. *W-10* was aboard during the journey.

W-8 was one of the aircraft which was frequently used aboard HNLMS De Ruyter. *Unfortunately, logbooks have not survived the war, making it difficult to determine which aircraft were aboard which ships.*
(Collection: Navy Museum Den Helder)

Two machines aboard HNLMS De Ruyter, Surabaya port. The photograph was taken in 1938.

During the fleet review on 6 September 1938, five Fokker C.XIw were part of the aerial display. Six newly delivered Dornier Do 24 flying boats are flanked by six Fokker T.IVA floatplanes.(Collection: Navy Museum Den Helder)

Bottom:
A snapshot taken from the rear cockpit during the aerial display
(Collection: P. Korbee)

CAMOUFLAGE TRIALS

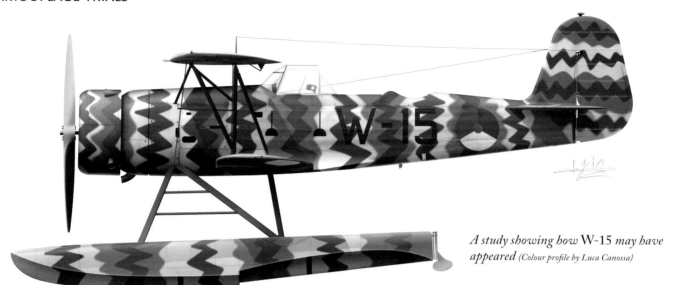

A study showing how W-15 *may have appeared* (Colour profile by Luca Canossa)

In 1936, some attention was given to aircraft camouflage. Two Fokker T.IV float-plane bombers were painted in disruptive patterns of various tones of grey. A more elaborate study on aircraft visibility during various conditions was conducted during the following year. It was concluded that application of camouflage patterns did not reduce the effectiveness of stereoscopic rangefinders. The main goal of camouflaging an aircraft should be obscuring it from view while in the air. Brightly painted lower surfaces (white or aluminium) were most effective when observed from sea level, while a different hue was advised for the upper surfaces – which would most likely be seen with the sea as background.

Both pages:
W-15 *after being lowered into the water and preparing for take-off. The disruptive paint job is clearly visible in these photos.*
(Collection: Navy Museum Den Helder)

A port-side view of W-15. *In the background are HNLMS* De Ruyter *and another ship anchoring.*
(Collection: T. Postma)

Left:
A rather blurry photo, but the only known view at the starboard side of the camouflaged W-15.
(Collection: T. Postma)

Although earlier experiments concluded that camouflage patterns were not found effective, three Fokker C.XIw aircraft were used for further experiments. The aircraft involved – W-5, W-6, and W-15 – received different variants of a disruptive pattern in two colours which were applied over the regular aluminium dope finish. The colourful rudder was painted over during the trials, and the floats seem to have been painted aluminium before the camouflage pattern was applied. The exact colours are not known, but the lighter of the two appears to have similar value and saturation as the *Hollandgrau* which was applied on the float struts. The darker paint of the two appears to have been a dark green or very dark grey.

When the modern Dornier Do 24K flying boats were delivered a new paint scheme was accepted. The upper surfaces of the wing and tail plane and fuselage surfaces above the waterline of these aircraft were painted *Hollandgrijs* (or Hollandgrau, RLM 02). The lower surfaces of the wing, tail planes and fuselage were first painted aluminium. This scheme was called

Ikarol A. It was modified by changing the aluminium undersides with light grey (*licht Hollandgrijs*, or *Hollandgrau hell*). This scheme was called Ikarol B, and was also used on the newly purchased aircraft series. Fokker T.VIIIw and Fokker C.XIVw aircraft series.

W-15 *aboard NHLMS* Java.
(Collection: Navy Museum Den Helder)

And W-12, *perched on the port side of HNLMS* Java.
(Collection: Navy Museum Den Helder)

W-12, *photographed from the rear cockpit of* **W-15.** *The small registry is just visible below the tail plane.* (Collection: Navy Museum Den Helder)

Given the earlier conclusions, it is unclear why the experimental schemes were tested, and with what purpose in mind. A short statement remains, which explains that the aircraft needed to be obscured from view both on the water and in coastal areas when the aircraft were on prolonged patrol duties…

Most, if not all, photos of the camouflaged aircraft were made during a regular naval exercise, which took place between 6 September 1938 and 13 October 1938, when both HNLMS *Java* and *De Ruyter* were taking part in a regular naval exercise. The photos have survived in a photo album compiled by navy officer H. de Jonge van Ellemeet. He arrived from Holland on 20 October 1938, and embarked on *Java* on the same day. Although he was an avid photographer, it is possible the photos of the camouflaged aircraft were taken by someone else.

During the exercise, *W-12* and *W-15* were aboard HNLMS *Java*. While *W-15* was painted in a disruptive camouflage pattern, *W-12* also featured non-standard markings. The tail rudder had been painted over with aluminium dope, and a second, smaller registry was placed directly below the horizontal tail plane.

A curious incident occurred during the exercise. The Dutch navy was confronted with a new threat which would be a concern during the coming years. Japanese fishing ships were often actively gathering military information and were equipped with long-range radio equipment. The C.XIw crews would be frequently searching for these spy ships. On 30 September, a Japanese fishing ship was evading examination and was actually hit when it was fired at as a warning.

Destroyer HNLMS Van Galen *seen from* **W-15.** (Collection: Navy Museum Den Helder)

W-12 *with Admiral-class destroyer*
HNLMS Van Ghent *in the background.*

(Collection: Navy Museum Den Helder)

HNLMS *Java* collided with another ship on
13 October and had to be repaired. These
repairs lasted until 26 December 1938.[*]

---

[*] The earlier mentioned H. de Jonge van Ellemeet
arrived in the Netherlands Indies while HNLMS
Java was in dock.

The camouflage trials may have continued
after these repairs had been completed.
But *W-5* was lost when it was hoisted
aboard HNLMS *Java* on 4 January 1939.
The hook carrying the plane broke and the
fuselage was buckled beyond repair. The
crew escaped with minor injuries.

Two intriguing photos of W-6, showing a different camouflage pattern compared to W-15. The bottoms of the wings appear not to be painted in a camouflage pattern.

(Via K. Kalkman)

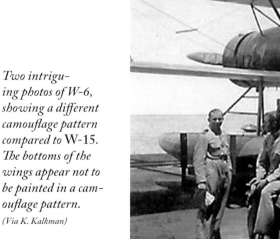

Only a single photo of the camouflaged W-5 *is known. Here while lifted aboard HNLMS* Java. *It was damaged beyond repair during such a hoisting operation on 4 January 1939.*

Left: *This photo reveals the underside of the wings were also camouflaged.* (Collection: Navy Museum Den Helder)

It is not entirely clear if the trials were continued after the loss of *W-5*. Three C.XIw aircraft are seen in the pre-war movie *'t sal waerachtig wel gaen'*, which was filmed during February 1939 and premiered on 1 February 1940. Several scenes were filmed at MVK Morokrembangan. In one scene, *W-1* is seen on a ramp, ready to be rolled into the water. Two other C.XIw can be seen. One is seen while being pushed out of a hangar. Although the shot focuses on the floats and lower part of the fuselage, its camouflage pattern is clearly visible. A third C.XIw is seen behind the *W-1*, head-on, in the background. This must have been *W-15*.

Centre:
W-1 *seen on the ramp of MVK Morokrembangan. On the right the nose of* W-6, *and in the background a head-on view of* W-15.
(Movie still from 't sal waerachtig wel gaen'
Collection: Netherlands Institute for Military History)

Bottom:
W-6 *while being pushed out of the main hangars at MVK Morokrembangan. The floats appear to have been painted in three different tones of paint.*
(Movie still from 't sal waerachtig wel gaen'
Collection: Netherlands Institute for Military History)

In the first weeks after Germany's attack on Poland, HNLMS De Ruyter was employed as flagship of the squadron patrolling the eastern part of the Netherlands Indies. A period of enforcing neutrality, patrols and exercises started, which lasted up to the first week of October. W-4 was embarked during this period. It is seen here aboard, and while launched.

(Collection: T. Postma. Bottom: Collection Navy Museum Den Helder)

MOBILISATION AND WARTIME OPERATIONS

Defence of the Netherlands Indies mobilised on 2 September 1939. The navy was split into two squadrons, each with a light cruiser (with two Fokker C.XIw aboard), plus three or four destroyers and a similar number of submarines. Each squadron could count on a GVT equipped with three Dornier Do 24 long-range patrol flying boats, supported by an aircraft mother ship. An intense period started, which was mostly spent with monitoring shipping, patrols, and exercises.

During September 1939, HNLMS *Java* was guarding the sea lanes west of Java and was patrolling vast areas of the Karimata Straits (Southernly Chinese Sea between Sumatra and Borneo). During these patrols, tragedy struck on 26 September. The fleet was anchored north of Banka Island (near Sumatra). After it had delivered the mail to shore, *W-7* was destroyed in a landing accident. Pilot officer 2nd class H.J. Stoutjesdijk was killed, while the observer received minor injuries.

From late September to the end of December, the engines of six aircraft were changed. The Cyclone F52 were switched for Cyclone F2 engines. Little is known about the whereabouts of individual aircraft. The shipborne aircraft were part of GVT 13 and 14, while those which remained at MVK Morokrembangan were used almost non-stop for training purposes.

W-8 *accompanies a Dornier Do 24. These large three-engined flying boats took over the long-range reconnaissance role from the Dornier Wal and Fokker T.IV types.*
(Collection: N. Braas)

A Fokker T.IVA floatplane, with its crew looking at the camera. They seem oblivious to the C.XIw pulling a loop behind them! *(Collection: Navy Museum Den Helder)*

W-10, *photographed during autumn 1939.*
Similar to the aircraft in Holland, the tail planes of the aircraft were painted over to decrease visibility. This was recorded in a decree dated 13 July 1939, and was to be effective per 12 October 1939. In practice, many tail planes had already been painted over before 12 October 1939.

(Collection: T. Postma)

HNLMS Tromp *arrived in the port of Batavia on 20 September, with* W-10 *aboard. She immediately joined the other patrolling ships. In WWII, this ship became one of the most succesful units of the Royal Netherlands Navy. The wooden frame at her side was used for gunnery exercises.* (Collection: Navy Museum Den Helder)

W-5 *embarked on* HNLMS Tromp.

(Collection T. Postma)

In the period after the fall of the Netherlands the navy was given convoy tasks to protect shipping against possible German raiders, which were active in the area. The MLD, in particular the Dornier Do 24 groups, were actively patrolling the sea ways and remote regions of the Netherlands Indies archipelago. After the Netherlands had capitulated, many new challenges arose. Training of new crew could no longer take place in the Netherlands, and there were no training aircraft available in the Netherlands Indies. Delivery of Dornier Do 24 aircraft was cut short. In a brief period, orders were placed for 48 Ryan STM-2 trainer aircraft, 48 Douglas DB-7C land-based torpedo bombers[*] and 36 Consolidated PBY Catalina flying boats. Ten Fokker C.XIVw float plane trainer aircraft could be diverted via the United Kingdom.

The Dutch navy, with its limited number of ships was now active not only in Netherlands Indies waters, but also from Rabaul (New Britain) to the Timor Sea (between Timor and Australia) and the southern Chinese Sea. Few details about C.XIw operational use during this period are known, but a memorandum dated 24 July 1940 states that a stock of 8,000 machinegun rounds and 80 50 kg bombs should be aboard HNLMS *Java* (although

---

[*] None were delivered: instead 32 DB-7B aircraft were allotted to the Netherlands Indies.

the Fokker C.XIw could not carry a bomb load). When HNLMS *Java* was on patrol duties she was photographed several times. She carried two C.XIw floatplanes in November 1940, and while visiting the Solomon Islands during early 1941.

During the last week of February 1941 Dutch navy ships were ordered to look out for the German heavy cruiser *Admiral Scheer*. It was feared this ship would be hunting merchant ships in the waters of Netherlands Indies. Two machines were aboard HNLMS *Java* when she left Surabaya port. HNLMS *De Ruyter* was also carrying two aircraft but remained in the Java Sea. After the threat had passed, HNLMS *Java* steamed to Suva (Fiji Islands). At Port Villa, New Hebrides, the float-planes circled above the harbour when the ship had to bunker fuel.

The roundel was replaced by the orange triangle markings. The markings had to be replaced by 1 December 1939. W-13 *is seen here.*

(Collection: T. Postma)

W-6 *with the large orange triangle markings and a combination of large and small registry. The larger version was painted over later on.*

(Colour profile by Luca Canossa)

The W-6 *was lost on 7 August 1940 during a training flight at MVK Morokrembangan.*

(Collection: T. Postma)

HNLMS De Ruyter *carrying two Fokker C.XIw, with the orange triangle markings.* (Collection: Netherlands Institute for Military History)

HNLMS *De Ruyter* was ordered to search for the Italian raiding sloop *Eritrea* (2,170 tons displacement), which was thought to be passing through Netherlands Indies waters. After a month of continuous patrolling, the Italian ship seemed to have vanished. *W-13* was lost in a fatal flying accident during a training flight at MVK Morokrembangan on 17 June 1941. Crew H.A.V.R. Baron van Lawick and J. Anzenberger were killed. After the loss of this fifth aircraft, only eight remained in service. This threatened to bring training and shipborne operations to a halt. An emergency purchase of 24 Vought OS2U-1 Kingfisher was rushed through in August 1941. Twelve of these would be used for training, while the other twelve would be embarked on ships. The aircraft were already en route to Java but were diverted to Australia when the Netherlands Indies capitulated.

When the Australian cruiser HMAS *Sydney* did not arrive at Freemantle harbour as planned, she was reported missing on 24 November. HNLMS *Tromp* was ordered to join the search for the Australian ship. During the searches, *W-14* suffered wing damage

HNLMS Tromp, *anchored at Port Moresby, New Guinea, 4 March 1941.*

(Naval History and Heritage Command, NH 80909)

Vought OS2U-1 Kingfisher with Dutch markings, photographed in a warehouse of Dade Bros, New York.
(Collection: P. Staal)

and was unable to continue flying until it could be repaired ashore.

During the search, rafts with German sailors were found, which turned out to be survivors of the German auxiliary cruiser *Kormoran*. Investigation resulted in the disbelief that HMAS *Sydney* was sunk by *Kormoran* on 19 November. The German raider, camouflaged as a regular merchant ship, was intercepted by HMAS *Sydney* off the coast of Western Australia. The *Kormoran* caught the unsuspecting cruiser by surprise. During the ensuing battle, HMAS *Sydney* was heavily damaged and eventually sank. After the confrontation *Kormoran* was crippled and later scuttled by its crew.

The orange nationality markings were modified during July 1941; the tail rudders were painted over, again, in aluminium coloured paint. The triangles on the top wings were painted over as well, and the triangles on the fuselage sides were reduced in size, to roughly 1/3 of the original size. The black borders on these triangles were reduced in width. The large black registries were painted over, and new smaller examples were painted beneath the horizontal tail planes. (Collection: Netherlands Institute for Military History)

WAR WITH JAPAN

After a period of maintaining strict neutrality, the Netherlands Indies were dragged into war on 8 December 1941. The Netherlands Fleet Air Arm (MLD) was not at full strength yet and counted the following aircraft;

Training;
47 Ryan STM-2
10 Fokker T.IVA
10 Fokker C.XIVw

Reconnaissance
35 Dornier Do 24
28 Consolidated PBY Catalina
8 Fokker C.XIw

Fokker C.XIw's appeared during the aerial parade in honour of Queen Wilhelmina's 61st birthday. The Fokker T.IVA and Ryan STM-2 aircraft are camouflaged in khaki green paint. The Fokker C.XIw's may have been painted in a similar way during the final months of their service. (Collection: Navy Museum Den Helder)

HNLMS *Java* was on a visit in Australia, carrying two aircraft. She was rushed to Singapore on 9 January 1942 and commenced patrolling and escort duty. She was later joined by HNLMS *De Ruyter* and *Tromp*. During this period, Singapore was visited several times. According to an eyewitness account, HNLMS *Java*'s Fokker C.XIw floatplanes were disembarked at Singapore at some point in time, because it was feared they might obstruct the field of fire of the two 15 cm guns which were placed in front and aft of the deck where the aircraft were stowed. Moreover, the aircraft were considered a fire hazard during combat. And lastly, lowering the aircraft by crane would make the ship vulnerable to submarine attacks.

HNLMS *De Ruyter* was at anchor in a sheltered position between the islands of Lombok and Sumbawa. Here, the ship was prepared for war. All equipment which was considered unnecessary was tossed overboard. Curiously, the stock of aviation fuel for the Fokkers was dumped as well! Little is known about aircraft use during the coming months, but the scarce snippets of information give the impression that aircraft were aboard on several dates. HNLMS *De Ruyter* was painted in camouflage colours during a short docking between 18 and 26 December. One photo shows the ship, camouflaged, carrying two C.XIw floatplanes.

HNLMS Java *in disruptive camouflage, which was applied soon after 8 December 1941. The ship is carrying aircraft, although a censor tried to obscure them in the picture. (Collection: Netherlands Institute for Military History)*

HNLMS **De Ruyter** *was painted with a camouflage scheme during the first half of December 1941. She is seen here carrying two aircraft.* (Museums Victoria)

In the weeks following December 7th, the commands of American, British, Dutch, and Australian forces were unified in ABDACOM, in an effort to consolidate defence against Japan. Command of the Dutch fleet would be absorbed in ABDAFLOAT. The reconnaissance tasks were now made the responsibility of the Dornier Do 24 and PBY Catalina crews, and aircraft of the allied forces. The Dutch fleet was, in this way, robbed of its own long range reconnaissance capability. Direct communication between ships and aircraft was made impossible due to the new hierarchy in command, and in some cases due to technical reasons. On 1 February, available navy ships joined in the Combined Striking Force (CSF), which was commanded by Dutch rear admiral Karel Doorman.

While the campaign unfolded, the remaining C.XIw floatplanes were transferred to MVK Morokrembangan and used for reconnaissance tasks and as training aircraft in the direct area around the base. Two machines – *W-4* and *W-10* – were shot ablaze by Japanese aircraft on 2 February during a heavy attack on MVK Morokrembangan.

HNLMS *De Ruyter* kept at least one aircraft aboard during the first half of February. In fact, Doorman sent a written message by plane to his commander, stating his intention to evacuate the ships under his command to Australia. This was urgently forbidden in February – the entire CSF was needed for the defence of the Netherlands Indies.

HNLMS *De Ruyter* was photographed on 14 February 1942 while she was moored in Lampung Bay (Southern Sumatra). She was photographed with her two C.XIw aboard. HNLMS *De Ruyter* was in action in the Gaspar Strait on 15 February, but there is no information on plane use. Shortly afterwards, the planes must have left and flown to MVK Morokrembangan.

W-12 was shot down on 18 February. It was intercepted by a group of Mitsubishi A6M fighters, which had been strafing Maospati airfield in the east of Java. Three pilots of the 2nd Shotai engaged the lonesome Fokker, somewhere between the airfield and the town of Cepu. None other than Saburo Sakai mentioned in his log; *"en route to Malang we encountered a Dutch floatplane and I broke formation long enough to send him crashing into the ocean."*
Malang is located in eastern Java, almost 200 km east of Maospati, and 50 km south of Surabaya, and some 50 km from the shore. The exact location of this interception is not clear. Both crewmen were able to bail out, but tragically, observer van der Boom had no parachute. He tried to hold on to his pilot but could not cling on and fell to his death.

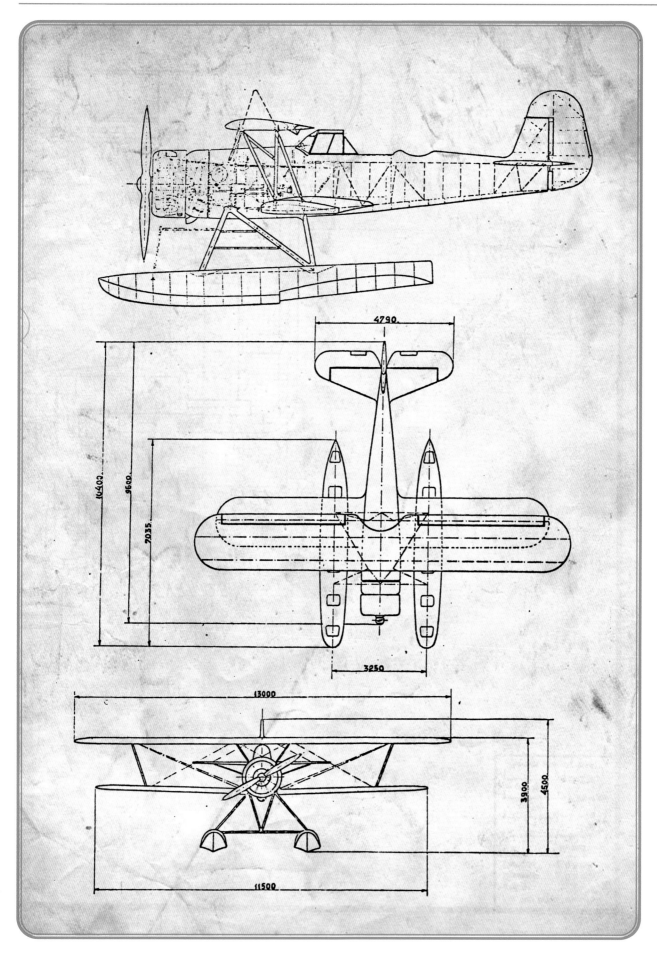

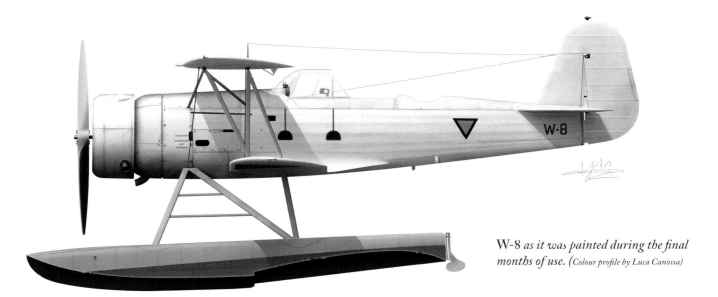

W-8 *as it was painted during the final months of use.* (Colour profile by Luca Canossa)

As mentioned earlier, the Dutch Navy light cruisers were sent into battle without their floatplanes aboard. This rather short-sighted decision left the ships fighting without their early warning and scouting abilities. This resulted in various close calls where Dutch navy squadrons were within striking distance of Japanese transports or other naval units. The lack of observation aircraft proved to be a handicap during the events leading to the Battle of Badung Strait on 19 February, during which an opportunity to intercept a Japanese fleet of transport ships heading for Bali was missed. Instead, three short night confrontations with Japanese escort ships were made, resulting in the loss of destroyer HNLMS *Piet Hein.*

BATTLE OF THE JAVA SEA

After the skirmish in Badung Strait a large-scale Japanese air offensive against targets on Java started. An invasion seemed inevitable. Based on intercepted Japanese radio transmissions, an invasion of Java was predicted to take place on 27 February.

This prediction proved to be correct. An allied fleet of two heavy cruisers, three light cruisers and nine destroyers was ordered to search for and destroy a large Japanese convoy. The Allied ships intercepted a Japanese fleet of two heavy cruisers, two light cruisers and fourteen destroyers, which protected a fleet of ten transport ships. During the actual confrontation with the Japanese fleet, a lack

of communication between the British, American, Australian, and Dutch ships, combined with a lack of aerial reconnaissance proved to be fatal for the Allied ships. During a first clash at daytime, Doorman tried to avoid a direct confrontation with the Japanese cruisers. His manoeuvring may have been misunderstood by the captains aboard the other ships. The lack of observing aircraft severely limited the Allied overview of the situation. Japanese aircraft, on the other hand, continuously observed every Allied move. During the chaotic combat at night the Allied suffered heavy losses. The Dutch navy lost its cruisers HNLMS *De Ruyter* and *Java,* plus destroyer HNLMS *Kortenaer.* The British suffered the loss of

A Fokker C.XIw and a Ryan STM-2 seen at MVK Morokrembangan during the final weeks of war. Bamboo stakes were dug in as a precaution against enemy parachutists. A rather poor photo, but it is a last glance at the aircraft before its pitiful end.

W-6, photographed on 31st March 1937.
(Collection: T. Postma)

destroyers HMS *Electra* and *Jupiter,* while cruiser HMS *Exeter* was forced to retreat with heavy damage.

The Japanese invasion of Java commenced without much delay. Only five C.XIw aircraft now remained. *W-1, W-8, W-11, W-14,* and *W-15* were flown to support base Lengkong, located on the river Brantas, some 90 kilometres south-west of MVK Morokrembangan. Eight remaining Fokker T.IVa floatplanes were diverted to Lengkong as well. To prevent them falling into Japanese hands, the aircraft were scuttled on 2 March 1942. A week later, the bitter fighting ceased. The Netherlands Indies capitulated on the 9th.

FOREIGN SALES

The C.XIw was mentioned in the sales brochures from 1936 onwards. Information sheets were published in French and English. A variant with a Bristol Perseus III engine was described in a performance sheet dated 1 December 1938.

During the second half of the 1930s, Fokker representatives invested much time and energy in presenting the current types C.X, D.XXI, T.V, G.I and T.VIIIw to foreign armed forces. The Fokker C.XIw was also pitched to several potential customers; France, Denmark, Norway, Finland, and Sweden received documentation. But these countries were looking for aircraft with torpedo carrying capabilities, or twin-engine types. During September 1938, Fokker offered a series of nine Fokker C.XIw floatplanes to the Portuguese navy. This did not result in an order. The Netherlands Fleet Air Arm (MLD) would turn out to be the only operator of the sturdy floatplane.

W-2 was lost while embarked on HNLMS Java. *The aircraft was damaged beyond repair on 18 July 1938 when it was being hoisted aboard. (Collection: T. Postma)*

Aircraft	First flight	Acceptance flight(s)	Fate
W-1 (5399)	20 July 1935		Scuttled 2 March 1942
W-2 (5420)	11 February 1937	17, 18, 24 February 1937	W/O 18 February 1938
W-3 (5421)	10 March 1937	23, 24 March 1937	Destroyed 10 May 1940
W-4 (5422)	7 April 1937	27, 29, 30 April, 5, 8 May 1937	Destroyed 2 February 1942
W-5 (5423)	14 May 1937	20, 24 May, 3 June 1937	W/O 4 January 1939
W-6 (5424)	28 May 1937	1 June 1937	W/O 7 August 1940
W-7 (5425)	31 May 1937	3 June 1937	W/O 26 September 1939
W-8 (5426)	19 July 1937	4, 23 August 1937	Scuttled 2 March 1942
W-9 (5427)	14 July 1937	23 August 1937	W/O 13 April 1940
W-10 (5461)	10 September 1937	8 October 1937	Destroyed 2 February 1942
W-11 (5462)	27 September 1937	8 October 1937	Scuttled 2 March 1942
W-12 (5463)	1 November 1937	30 November 1937	Shot down 18 February 1942
W-13 (5464)	10 November 1937	30 November 1937	W/O 17 June 1941
W-14 (5465)	15 December 1937	18 January 1938	Scuttled 2 March 1942
W-15 (5466)	12 December 1937	18 January 1938	Scuttled 2 March 1942

A RECOVERY ATTEMPT

During the late 1990s, a group of enthusiastic Dutch historians and archaeologists ambitiously searched for the lost Fokker C.XIw and Fokker T.IVA wrecks on the site they were scuttled in the Brantas river. The project revived interest in the pre-war naval Fokker aircraft but the expedition did not find any trace of the aircraft.

Author	Publisher
Edwin Hoogschagen	Walburg Pers / Lanasta
Graphic design	**Translation Revision**
Jantinus Mulder	Deben Translations

First print, February 2024
ISBN 978-94-6456-154-8
e-ISBN 978-94-6456-155-5

NUR 465

Contact Warplane:
jantinusmulder@walburgpers.nl

Lanasta

© 2024 Walburg Pers / Lanasta

www.walburgpers.nl/lanasta

DEDICATED TO THE MEMORY OF
PETER KORBEE
(24-2-1946 – 23-2-2023)
THANK YOU PETER, FOR YOUR
ENTHUSIASM AND FRIENDSHIP.
BLUE SKIES!

Thanks
Navy Museum Den Helder, Museums Victoria, Dutch National Archives, Aviodrome, Wolter Bonkestooter, Nico Braas (†), Luca Canossa, Frits Gerdessen, John Greuter, Jan Grisnich, Coen van den Heuvel, Karel Kalkman, Peter Korbee (†), Jantinus Mulder, Ronnie Olsthoorn, Thijs Postma, Martin Smit, Prudent Staal.

Pictures: from the author's collection, unless stated otherwise.

Sources
- Fokker archives, Aviodrome, Lelystad airport
- Delpher newspaper archives www.delpher.nl
- Anten, J., et al, *Hr.Ms. Kruisers Java en Sumatra*, Asia Minor, 2001
- Bruin, de, R., et al, *Illusies en incidenten*, Koninklijke Luchtmacht, 1988
- Elias, P.J., *Dan liever de lucht in*, P.N. van Kampen & Zoon N.V., 1963
- Geldhof, N. *Verkennen en bewaken – Dornier Do 24K vliegboten van de Marineluchtvaartdienst*, Afdeling Maritieme Historie, Ministerie van defensie, 1979
- Geldhof, N. *Fokkers katapultvliegtuig C.XI-w*, Avia June 1984
- Geldhof, N., *Fokker's kruiservliegtuig C.XI-w*, *Luchtvaart*, January 1997
- Gerdessen, F., *Fokker C.15-W*, *Luchtvaartkennis*, 2016 nummer 3
- Greuter, J.H.N., et al, *Camouflage en kentekens op vliegtuigen van de Nederlandse strijdkrachten*, Bonneville, 1997
- Koppen, P.L., *De vliegtuigkatapult aan boord van Hr.Ms. de Ruyter*, *Marineblad*, January 1939
- Legemaate, H.J., Mulder, A.J.J., van Zeeland, M.G.J et al, *Hr.Ms. Kruiser de Ruyter 1933-1942*, Asia Minor, 1999
- Shores, C., Cull, B., and Izawa, Y., *Bloody Shambles volume two*, Grub street, 1993
- Teitler, G., *De strijd om de slagkruisers 1938-1940*, De Bataafsche Leeuw, 1984